Testimonies of Faith

A collection of stories of God's interaction with man.

By The Writers of Faith

Dedication

We believe the single most compelling, necessary characteristic to personal evangelism is a Christ lived life. Everyone who is trying to live a Christ lived life will have at least this one thing in common; that is a testimony.

We dedicate this collection of testimonies to those who don't have one. We hope and pray that this book finds its way into the hands of those who don't know the glorious wonder of living a Christ-like life. All of the stories in this book are a first-hand account of how God has intervened in the life of man. If there is one commonality that flows from story to story, it is the love of God. In every story, you will see the extended hand of the love of God to heal, save, deliver, and to live a better life after receiving salvation. In this book, you will find evidence of our living God but more than that we hope you can see that He wants you to know His love.

Table of Contents

Section III: Healing 40

Section IV: Before and After 51

Section V: Conclusion 65

DELIVERANCE

†

"The righteous cry, and the Lord heareth, and delivereth them out of all their troubles."

Psalms 34:17 KJV

He Just Laughed and Told Me Tough
By Rev. Charles Reif, Lt. Col. USMC (Ret)

In April of 1970, I was halfway through my tour as an infantryman in Vietnam and the Assistant to the Sergeant-Major of the Headquarters Company. Because our battalion was changing positions, we had been deployed in the western part of II Corp and were repositioning eastward to a spot that overlooked what we commonly called VC Valley. I flew into the new position with the first rifle company that would be digging in the command bunkers and setting up the defensive perimeter. It was hot, dirty work, but at least we weren't out pounding the jungle.

I spent the day directing activity as more troops and supplies of all kinds were flown in: steel plating, huge oak beams, com and razor wire, not to mention the 5 105 howitzers and ammo....you name it. We set up on the very edge of a cliff that dropped off about 2000 feet to a v-shaped valley below. We were on the west side with mountains about 2000 feet above our elevation on the east side and about a half-mile across. It was getting dark and I heard the call for the last helicopter heading out for the night; so, I jumped onboard and waited, alone. Then, I saw our Battalion Commander (XO) and our Sergeant Major approaching the helicopter. The Sergeant Major motioned for me to get off; he told me that I wasn't coming on this bird, and smiled. I asked why. He just laughed and told me, "tough."

I stood there as the three of them took off with empty seats. The Sergeant Major was looking at me and grinning. He was punishing me because he didn't like my boss.

The helicopter rose to a hover while I was asking God why. I needed to get back. I didn't understand...but, I trusted in Him. Satan was screaming at me to get angry; instead, I started to praise the Lord and thank Him for

4

stranding me there for the night. My life scripture is Romans 8:28, "And we know that all things work together for good to those who love God, to those who are the called according to His purpose."

The bird turned and then dove over the cliff. I watched as the pilot descended, trading altitude for airspeed, then near the bottom he began his pullout. I looked at the climbing helicopter starting its turn back towards us. Immediately, the jungle erupted. Three Soviet anti-aircraft machine guns opened fire and green tracers leaped out of the dark jungle arching upward hitting the helicopter.

The bird exploded into a flaming fireball, slowly tumbling earthward. Time completely stopped! Moments before I was marooned, the next, I was alive. Everyone was looking at me. All that came to my mind was, "Thank you, Lord." All night the scene played in my mind over and over again, the Lord reminding me that He is my shield. Stay behind Him. Follow His leads. When in doubt, Praise Him! He will lead.

My Husband
By Nelidi Torres

It was February 2002 when I married Jose Cernada Sr. On February 20, 2002, he crossed the Canadian border into the USA to witness the birth of his only son, Jose Cernada Jr., born that day at 11:35 PM. I had no idea what I was getting myself into. He not only abused me in all forms. He also abused our son.

We lived an incredibly sad, fearful life. I was miserable and my son was extremely depressed. We didn't have family or friends who would visit us. We were lonely, isolated and didn't have contact with anyone. My husband was living two separate lives. Monday through Thursday he was a husband and father. Friday through Monday he lived the single life.

When my son was in second grade, I was diagnosed with thyroid cancer, which turned out to a blessing from God. Despite the multiple surgeries I underwent, and despite my legal blindness, God was able to use my circumstances to liberate me from my husband. It was difficult, but I slowly started to hear and obey God's voice. I had no idea that God was a person and alive, with a voice and feelings. I didn't know that He alone had solutions I had never contemplated.

God blessed me with SSI and relocated me from New York City to Florida and He provided me with a brand new townhouse. My son began attending Faith Christian Academy with a Step Up Scholarship. He also serves God every Sunday as the cameraman in the sanctuary. God introduced me to Godly women who aided me in my divorce. God even paid for my divorce. I was granted a free divorce due to my circumstances. I received the divorce decree four years ago on Christmas Eve; that is how I know God paid for it. He also removed my son and I from a sad, depressing, frightening life and introduced us to what life with Christ could be.

I serve God faithfully at Faith of Assembly God. It is my home away from home. In 2016, I attended a symbolic ceremony where I married God. Though it was symbolic, it had real implications for me as I willingly placed God in His proper place in my life. He is my husband, provider, leader, healer, and the love of my soul, my friend, and savior. In essence, He is my everything.

My son and I continue to grow, connect and serve at Faith Assembly Of God. We continue to speak and listen to God. And we know that everything we have, He has provided. We fellowship with Him every day and seek His counsel in all things. This is valuable to us because if we heed His Word, we will succeed. He may not give us an immediate answer, but in time, He will open the door for His promises to enter our lives. I am elated that He loved me first and that I answered His call, His soft whisper and His beautiful and unconditional love. Amen.

Section II:

SALVATION

✝

"For God so loved the world, that He gave his only begotten Son, that whosoever believeth in Him shall not perish, but have everlasting life."

John 3:16 KJV

Broken but Set Free
By Patty Pabon

I was born in Manhattan, New York and raised in the South Bronx. When I was a little girl, I attended church only on Easter and Christmas. But under the cover of night, my family and I followed a darker religion called Santeria, a cult-like practice that merges Catholicism with voodoo type ceremonies and saint worship. We sacrificed animals and bowed down to these so-called "powerful gods, our protectors." I saw manifestations of possessed people crawling like snakes, levitating and speaking in demonic tongues. My mother always told me not to look into their eyes or cross my legs and arms.

This was the way of life for us. At the age of fifteen, I was dedicated to an idol called, "Obatala." I was dressed in white and there was a huge ceremony of seven young girls. We had to drink a mixed potion, feed fruits to this doll looking idol and bow down and chant to receive power from the spirit. Deep down inside of me, I knew this was not right, but as an obedient child, I did what I was told. I saw normal-looking people turn ugly. They became like horrible people after the spirits took over their bodies.

I was tormented by these demons all of my life. I was bound by fear. And, soon after being dedicated to this idol, my life went downhill. Things happened to me that led me down the wrong path. This experience damaged me mentally, emotionally and spiritually, leaving me feeling unworthy, insecure, bitter and angry.

In October of 1994, my husband and I were invited to a play called, "Heaven's Gates, Hell's Flames" at Faith Assembly Church. That day we answered the altar call to receive Jesus as our Lord and Savior. The first five years were filled with demonic encounters, but through a spiritual encounter with Jesus, my journey at last brought me to a place of freedom. I have been saved now for over 22 years and all of my children are saved and serving in ministry.

The change that I experienced during that time developed into an immense stirring of my true calling. I found my passion in helping women find their true identity, break free from their past and live an abundant life. Having suffered throughout my childhood, I know first-hand what it is to be broken. If I can make it through it, then anyone can.

A Good Personal Crisis
By Carl Stephens

There's nothing like a good personal crisis to cause a change in direction. Mine happened at the age of 19. I was a young man entering into the brand new world of college.

I had been dating a girl for about a year and a half and thought I knew my plans for my life. At the time, I was majoring in Criminal Justice with my sights set on working for the FBI. Even though I was raised in the church with a fond affection for all things godly, I was not applying any of those things to my personal life. The girl I was dating was of good moral character, but she knew less about God than I although she had been raised in a good—but non-Christian—home. To my knowledge, she never attended church.

One Tuesday afternoon, I stopped by her house after classes, only to discover she had accepted a ride home from a guy that was obviously interested in her. In my unsaved state of mind, I lost it! Looking back now, that experience seems to have been the straw that broke the camel's back, so to speak. I was miserable and unhappy with a lot of things in my life. On top of this, I had discovered that my dad was living a secret, sinful life of alcohol and adultery.

Amazingly enough, God sometimes lets us go through a crisis to bring us to our senses. That was certainly the case that Tuesday afternoon when I drove away from my girlfriend's house. I pulled onto a side road I had never been on before, just to have a good cry and vent. With thoughts of just ending my life drifting through my mind, I looked up to see a small church a short distance down the road. It seemed the only thing to do at that moment—to go in and pour out my heart to God and ask him to help and forgive me. I left that church that day a changed man. How do I know? I had joy, peace, and overwhelming love—so much so that, the very next day, I passed that same young man on his way to see my girlfriend and I waved to him. That, my friend, was a miracle of God's grace and love.

If you're going through a crisis, let it lead you to the only One that can and will change your life forever: Jesus Christ.

Darkness to Light
Robert Adessa

I was born in Reykjavik, Iceland in 1953. My father
was a civil service employee at the Naval Air Station
Keflavik and my mother was Icelandic. We lived off base in
nearby Keflavik and it was there as a young lad, looking up
at the night sky, that I was filled with a sense of awe and
wonder at the utter vastness of the star-filled universe. I
instinctively knew there had to be a God, but I didn't know
Him. My parents made it a point to send their kids to
Catholic Sunday School and to go with us to Mass, but I
never made the connection that a loving God took a personal
interest in me.

Years later, a nagging sense of emptiness was
warning me that I was walking deeper into darkness. There
was a veil over my eyes and I was unable to see my true
spiritual condition. One night at Keflavik, I had gathered
with some friends for a party. As we sat around a coffee
table, I had a sudden open vision of Jesus Christ on the cross
and was enveloped by an unconditional love that was as
deep and wide as the heavens. My immediate response was
to run, even as God's love touched my heart and brought me
to tears. I abruptly stood up, walked out of the apartment and
got into the car. I just sat in the car pondering what I had just
seen and marveling at the amazing peace I felt in my heart.

About eleven months later, I was back in Florida,
and while I was raking the lawn of my parents' home in
Casselberry, I was approached by someone that explained
the Gospel to me and then asked if I wanted to be saved.
This time, I didn't run from the Lord, but repented of my
sins and believed that the Father had sent Jesus Christ to die
for me. The next day, I was taken to a Victory in Jesus
prayer meeting in Winter Park, Florida. The service opened
up with a praise song, "Oh, Let us Magnify the Lord." As
soon as I started singing, God's unconditional love starting

pouring into my heart, and when my tears finally stopped, my heart was as clean and white as snow. The Peace that passes understanding was guarding my heart and I've never felt such joy. The Pastor called me up front and prayed with me, and then asked me to hand him the pack of cigarettes that were in my shirt pocket. Not only did God save me on that November day in 1976, but he instantly removed my addiction to tobacco. The Lord had turned my night to day, and my life had a new found freedom. My heart and disposition had changed and the things of the world were dimmed as I fed on the Bible and learned to trust the Lord.

Again Jesus spoke to them, saying, "I am the light of the world. Whoever follows me will not walk in darkness, but will have the light of life." John 8:12 ESV

The Truth Will Set You Free
By Gabrielle Triyono

I've called myself a Christian for almost my whole life, but it wasn't until January 2014 that I could say I had truly accepted Jesus as my Lord. Before that, I only knew who God was because I had grown up in church since childhood. I heard about Him from sermons preached by my pastor, stories from Sunday school and my family. Although all these things were great, it did nothing for me because I had never found Jesus myself.

Jesus was never my Lord and was nothing more than a God who created me. All I knew to do was to believe He existed so I would go to heaven. That was my version of salvation for most of my life. I was Lord over my own life, choosing to do the things that I wanted to do and neglecting to follow the truth of God. It wasn't until January 2014, when I found myself sitting at my University, feeling desperate, trapped and lost, that my own life choices started to cause more troubles. The next thing I knew, I was in the deepest pit of my life with no hope.

I was chained and imprisoned by my own actions. I didn't know what else to do or who else to turn to. But, it was at that moment that God reminded me of a verse that truly changed my life. It was John 8:32, which says, "Then you will know the truth, and the truth will set you free." I needed to be set free and Jesus seemed like the only one I could run to. So that day, I decided to lay down my life and give it up to Christ.

That was the best decision I ever made. It was when I laid down my life that I truly found Him. I had finally met Christ personally and started my journey following Him, choosing to let Him be Lord over my life. Following His truth involved going through trials and pains, but it was worth it because that was when I found real hope in my life. He broke my chains and slowly I started to see His truth set me free, just as the verse said it would. My life began to turn around, into something beautiful.

God has a beautiful story for you. Will you let Him write it? Will you make Him Lord over your life? We all have a story. But, the best story can only happen when God writes it. Trust that He will be the best author of your life. He is my hope, and He can be your hope as well.

I Am a New Creation in Christ
By Michael C. James

When I was in Junior High School, I was attending church at the invitation of the pastor's son. At the church, a prison evangelist was sharing the Word of God. I heard him explain how to be saved from the Bible. To me, the message was exciting and thrilling. It answered the most important question on my mind, how to know salvation in Christ Jesus. I had never heard of this Good News in the Bible. I was a member of another church and they did not teach this message. My Church did not trust the Bible to have a life-saving message.

As I was listening to the evangelist, the image in my mind was convicting me. I saw myself as a young athlete climbing a gym rope to the ceiling. As I reached the top of the rope, there was no victory. I reached out trying to achieve success, and all I found was darkness and loss. I was separated from God by personal sin; I was trapped in sin, death, and false religion. I did not have eternal life. I did not know Jesus as my Lord and Savior.

I agreed with the Bible's message of salvation. I needed Jesus. I was sinful and spiritually empty, and He offered fulfillment and eternal life. He is the only bridge, light, and way to the Father. As I prayed to receive Jesus Christ, He enlightened the area of darkness and loss with His light at the top of the rope. With His forgiveness of my sin and my new life in Him, I am now a new person in Him. As the scripture states in 2 Corinthians 5:17 (KJV), "Therefore if any man be in Christ, he is a new creature: old things are passed away; behold, all things are become new."

I rejoice greatly in Christ, and in His supernatural life in me. As I look upward toward the sky, I am joining a cloud of witnesses exalting and praising Christ, my Lord and Savior.

My Son
By Silvia Torres

I was sexually abused at home at a very early age. As I grew up, I became rebellious and disorderly. Consequently, I made a lot of wrong choices during my life that led to my dysfunctional marriage. My son was heavily involved in drugs, and at one point, he was so devastated that he was walking the streets with his head hanging low, when he saw a flyer tossed on the ground. It read, "Are you tired of the way your life is going? Are you ready for a change?" So, he picked the flyer up and went to the address. It was a Christian church focused on drug rehabilitation.

He was interned there and when they allowed visitation, I went to see him. During Sunday service, I saw my son really involved in worship and even speaking in tongues. The next Sunday I showed up again, even though I didn't understand what was taking place, thinking that I was just going to show him my support. Little did I know, the Lord was directing my steps. I was broke and I needed healing. The Lord spoke to me and told me that all the time it was me He was looking for. He was bringing me to Him through my son. I broke down right there and accepted Jesus as my Lord and Savior.

During my Son's rehabilitation, he stayed at Victory Outreach Church until he became one of the leaders and eventually a Youth Pastor. I now have a healthy marriage, and my daughter, who was also involved in drugs, is also serving the Lord at her own church. We know that the Lord is not done with us yet. We are still a work in progress, but we have a different perspective on life, knowing that we have a purpose in Him.

Shambles
By Jean Presley

In 1977, my husband retired from the Air Force after twenty years of service. We had moved about 16 times to different parts of the United States. My husband was away from home a lot, so I was looking forward to settling down, buying a new house, new furniture and staying put. One thing I learned at that time was that things will never make a person happy. All my dreams were being fulfilled but I was so depressed and unhappy.

My life and family was in shambles. I was away from the Lord and I felt as though my marriage was over. My husband didn't have any interest in going to church. Almost every weekend we were out dancing and drinking, and I hated it. I was ready to call it quits. I was raised in church, so when I was at the bars, I felt shame and conviction.

I came home from work early one day and I turned on the TV just to drown out my thoughts. I couldn't find anything good to watch, so I began flipping through the channels and came across a program called The 700 Club. Pat Robertson and Ben Kinchlow were praying. They were asking people to accept Jesus as their Savior and I prayed and asked Jesus to forgive me for my sins. Instantly, the depression lifted! I did not tell my family or friends. I suppose I thought I would be a closet Christian. I felt wonderful for two or three days and then I began to feel the depression again. I had the TV on, watching the 700 Club, and I was praying and asking God why the depression was starting again. At that point, when I was ending my prayer, I raised my head and Ben Kinchlow was pointing at me. He said, "you need to tell someone." I have never had a prayer answered so fast.

I knew the one person I had to tell was my husband. I was convinced that he would leave when I asked him to go to church with me. This was going to be hard. When he got home from work, I asked him to come sit down because I needed to talk to him. I said that I wanted to go to church and he said he had never stopped me from going to church. I explained that I wanted to go to church as a family. I can't begin to explain the shock I felt when he agreed. We visited several churches and we decided to make Faith Assembly our church. That was over thirty-three years ago. My husband prays and reads his Bible every day. He has grown in his Faith and I am so thankful that God never gave up on us.

To all the ladies who have been praying for your husbands, my words would be: keep seeking and keep knocking. God is working on your behalf. It may get hard and you may think that it is not worth it, but I assure you it is. My marriage is wonderful (most days). My prayer is: Father God, in Jesus' Name, let this speak to someone's heart and give them encouragement.

Fatherly Love
By LaTanya Newell

I can remember living life feeling empty and seeking love in all the wrong places. I was looking for fatherly love and adoration because my father was absent from the home. I was going from relationship to relationship, and it started getting old. After experiencing the pain of an abusive relationship, I can remember a coworker reaching out to me and telling me that Jesus was the love of my life and wanted to be the father that I was seeking in others.

Accepting Him in my life has been the best decision EVER!!!

Change
By Lester Rector

I grew up in the gang-infested area of Cincinnati, Ohio. I found that, as a kid, if I were going to fit in, I would have to adapt to my environment. Socially, in order to be accepted and liked, I would have to become what others wanted me to be, never really accepting or loving who I was. As the years progressed, insecurity about myself, and even my talents as a musician and performer, caused me to feel as though I was stumbling through life, instead of actually living life with the confidence that every man and woman should have naturally. So, in the summer of 1992, I set out to make changes and personal goals that would help me to not only be a better man, but to have more confidence in myself. As I began living by those goals, I quickly realized that this was not what I was in need of, or in search of. In fact, I had no idea that what was about to happen to me that summer, would change my life forever, by giving me all I would need to fulfill all that I wanted for myself.

In July 1992, I went to a Southern Ohio State Church of God Youth Camp. Camp had always been a highlight for me, as it gave me the opportunity to enjoy some fun, social time while scouting for the next lady I would ask to the Friday night dance. This camp was different though. Instead of going to camp, this year I would be a camp counselor. What's funny about this is that everyone there knew that I was not a Christian. Going through the motions of being a camp counselor was somewhat easy because I grew up in church and knew enough about the rhetoric to get by. But, just as all things eventually come to a head, so did my charade – but not in the way you might think. You see, even though I was not a Christian, I had great respect for God and even found myself defending God as a kid and teenager. I was just trying to live my life and be accepted by people, doing whatever I needed to do in order to gain their approval. I never realized that all the approval I would need would come from God.

Friday night, the last night of camp was service as usual until the speaker, whose name I do not remember, got up to preach to the middle-school students. It was impactful. We were all captivated by the moment and the message being preached. At the end of his message he gave an altar call in which just about every student responded. Hundreds were at the altar. Students were "falling out" in the Spirit with no one touching them. Spiritual tongues could be heard resounding through the auditorium. And in the middle of that moment, God spoke to me. He said, "Lester, these students have something you do not have." Right there, I lifted my hands and said yes to Jesus, receiving Him as Lord and Savior of my life. The change I was trying to produce on my own had come from God and would forever be the foundation He would build upon for the rest of my life.

Life Is Better With Christ
By Roland Ranieri

I had always wondered why I was born and what my purpose in life was. I always knew there was a God but never had a relationship with Him. But, God had plan for me.

I was introduced to Faith Assembly of God by my daughter. It was her many Fine Arts and Worship Team practices that first brought me there, waiting in the car for her to finish. Then my wife started getting me to drive her to the church, which started me attending service here at Faith. At first, I would drop her off at church and then I would go home. Then, I started driving her and waiting for the service to finish. Eventually, I figured, why not go inside and see what's going on. I immediately fell in love with the music, the atmosphere, and the Word of God. I could feel the presence of God there.

I always thought that I didn't need to attend church, that I could take care of myself. But, then I accepted Jesus Christ into my life. And when I did, I knew that I had to serve my Lord by spreading the gospel and helping my fellow man. I've never gone through any significant hardships in my life and have always done well for myself, but after coming to Christ, my life went to a higher level. My marriage has gotten stronger, as we both serve Christ. My finances were blessed as I began to tithe. I have become a better father to my children, as now they can see the reflection of Jesus in me. I have been blessed to have many brothers in Christ. Whereas before, I only had a couple of close friends.

I was never interested in attending a Men's God Encounter. However, one day, my wife registered me and paid for my ticket using my money. I thought, now I have to go so I don't lose my money. At the Encounter, God spoke to me and I received the Holy Spirit. And, I gave my life to Christ. Thank God for my wife!

Now, I can't do enough for my Lord and Savior. I have become a part of the Men's Ministry at Faith, helping planning events and helping with registration. God also has blessed me by allowing me to lead the Men of Integrity group at the church so that we can come together as brothers in Christ to grow in our Faith. Now, I also participate as a group leader at our Men's God Encounters. I'm not sure why it took me so long in my life to come to Christ, but I know that He did it for a reason and that he has a plan for me. Thank you, Lord, for showing me what my purpose in life is. Thank you for loving me, caring for me, providing for me and for the promise of everlasting life.

Hell Is Hotter
By Michael Williams

My name is Michael Williams. I was born in Jesup, Georgia on November 27, 1987. I was born into a very religious family. My mom was a Pastor and my dad was a huge supporter of what she was doing. I have eight brothers and sisters that all grew up in our religious family.

Things were great until my mom decided to quit ministry. Once she quit being a Pastor, we stopped going to church. That happened when I was around the age of 8 or 9. A couple of years later, I started getting into really bad things, that I knew were wrong. But, I didn't care because it seemed like the right thing to do.

One day, I was invited to a youth service where everything changed. At the youth service, there was a bonfire. At the bonfire, we were roasting marshmallows and making s'mores, and as we were doing so, the Youth Pastor said, "I want to try something with you all really quick." I was thinking it would be something to do with the s'mores, but it was something different that would change my life. He said "I want you to stand as close to the fire as you can for as long as you can. Once you get too hot, step away. GO!" I stood there for maybe eight seconds and I stepped back because I thought my face was melting off...then my Youth Pastor said, "Can you imagine hell is hotter?"

After that, I gave my life to the Lord and a lot changed! After that season of my life, I began to get very involved in church. But, I was still living two very different lives. From age 13-18, I lived a double life that had me playing drums and involved in my church in one life. While my other life was filled with drugs and things I should have never been doing. Eventually, I became fed up with the double lifestyle and I moved to Orlando, Florida to pursue my calling in ministry. After making the decision to not only live for God, but also to work in ministry for God, my life became what it is today. It is a life that I know God is at the center of. God called me to fulltime ministry in Middle School but I never listened. It took me almost 6 years to finally obey that calling. But, that's when my life began to be the life that God intended for me to have.

And the Gift Goes On
By Minerva Davila

Hello. My name is Minerva. I am the fifth child of seven sisters. We were raised in South Chicago, where drugs, alcohol, and gangs were, and still are, common…All of us sisters did get caught up in the whirlwind of it all. But, by the grace of God we were all set free because one sister accepted Jesus Christ as her personal Lord and Savior and then came and shared her experience with me. When she first talked to me about being born again, I immediately told her she was in a cult.

As a former Catholic, I believed that the people who called themselves "born again" were in a cult. My sister laughed at my ignorance and began to explain it to me. She said it was in the Bible (John 3:3). She also told me about tithes and offering (Malachi 3:6-12) and how I could be set free from poverty! I could feel her passion about her new love. She then invited me to a Bible Study at her friend's home. I was a diehard Catholic! I went to church every Sunday. I knew the Father's name and did my communion etc. So, I told her I would go to the Bible Study but not to the church.

I went to the Bible Study and there I received Jesus Christ into my heart by the confession of faith (Romans 10:9-10). I didn't feel anything different. That day they were listening to a cassette tape teaching on Psalm 91 by John Osteen (Joel Osteen's dad). I will never forget that teaching! It's still stuck in my mind today so vividly and that was 27 years ago. It was a teaching about never giving up, and that is exactly what happened. I never gave up and was delivered of all the bondage (drugs, alcohol, and gangs) PRAISE GOD!

I was so excited with my new-found faith; I began telling others in the neighborhood what happened. They wanted to meet Jesus too! I started teaching Bible Studies in my home. And, many came to know Jesus Christ as their personal Lord and Savior as a result. I still teach in-home Bible Studies today because it had such an impact on my life! I also went out into the neighborhood to do street evangelism because I wanted everyone to hear my testimony about how good God is, in spite of where we live or where we're at in life. God came to seek and save the lost (Luke 19:10). And all I wanted to do was follow His Great Commission and to go into all the world… (John 16:15).

And the gift goes on! GOD IS SO GOOD!!!

Yukon Misadventure
By Dr. Richard Clawson

In November of 1975, I was an out-of-work commercial pilot. A friend of mine asked me to ferry an airplane from Penticton, British Columbia to Anchorage, Alaska. When I arrived in Penticton, there were scattered clouds and westerly winds. Most importantly, the weather at the next destination, Watson Lake, Yukon Territory, was forecast to be clear with unlimited ceilings.

Departing from Penticton, there was a temperature of minus 20 degrees. Flying northwest from there, the clouds got thicker and lower. I became aware that the clouds were partially covering the hills, but I was out of radio contact. I had to rely on the weather report I had received several hours ago from Penticton: unlimited ceiling and visibility at Watson Lake.

I proceeded to fly over a narrow mountain range and noted that the weather was getting worse. The flying weather was okay in the valley, but the mountains behind me became impassible because of the low clouds. I was not concerned because the weather was good at Watson Lake. On my way, I noticed an airport at a hunting campground. I made a mental note of the airport.

When I finally neared Watson Lake, I called the air traffic control tower, and the airport was weathered in. I had no choice but to go to the airport I had spotted at the hunting camp. It was getting dark as I landed. I walked into the camp and noticed several cabins. As I got closer, I noticed smoke coming from one of them. What luck! It was about minus 20 degrees there and the camp was not deserted. The caretaker was there alone all winter. He had no contact with the outside world and he did not need it.

The next day, I was ready to leave, but it was so cold that I could not start the engine; the battery was too weak after sitting outside for so long. Soon, a Canadian aircraft came searching for me, as I was overdue on my flight plan. The search pilot said he would send a rescue pilot with jumper cables to get me started. He also agreed to ask him to bring a bottle of whiskey for the caretaker. But, because of bad weather, the rescue pilot did not show up for five days.

I thoroughly enjoyed the next five days with the caretaker. I had never been to a hunting camp like this. Out front was a lake which was iced over. Outside was a cache (elevated pantry) to keep the food safe from bears. They could shimmy up the poles, but the floor of the cache was so wide they couldn't get on top of it. There was a ladder on the ground, but they never tried it. The caretaker hated wolves. Seeing one, he grabbed his rifle and took a shot from the door. He missed. The caretaker made the worst coffee I ever drank. He would dump the coffee grounds into a pan of water and heat it. It was free, though, so I did not complain. And, he was there when I really needed him.

The rescue pilot finally made it to the camp. I gave the caretaker the whiskey, and we jump-started my airplane. When I finally got to Watson Lake, Yukon Territory, I was humbled. I had escaped death. Five years later, I was saved. It was then, as a son of God, that I knew who saved me. God had me arrive at the only camp with a caretaker for miles around, knowing that the weather was worsening, it was deadly cold, my fuel was running low, and it was getting dark. Yes, I know my Jesus Christ saved me.

Praise the Lord!

Set Free
By Ruben Figueroa

As a child, God was introduced to me as a legalistic, unloving, overbearing, unforgiving entity. The religiosity I was raised in stressed the need to obey the law of God or be condemned to eternal damnation. As I grew older, the realization that I would never be able to meet the standard of full compliance, left me hopeless. As a result, at the age of 13, I checked out spiritually.

For the next eight to nine years, I did what I wanted. I wasn't a bad kid. My mother said I was the best of the seven of us. I loved baseball. But, I played anything with a bat, stick ball, even sponge ball. That was, until girls came into the picture. I chased the skirts and I played baseball. Then came alcohol, cigarettes and drugs.

I was raised in the ghettos of the South Bronx, New York in the 1970s. The drug culture was fully engaged, and everything that came with it was on full display, drugs on every corner, sex on the street and violent crime. My would-be mother-in-law was shot in a drive-by shooting. She lost a lung but survived.

In order to support my soon to be wife, I joined the Air Force and the drug use stopped. Through a series of God-inspired events, we ended up in Spokane Washington. But, the military seemed to encourage drinking, which being Puerto Rican, fit right in with my image of a Puerto Rican man. It was because of God's mercy I did not kill anyone while driving drunk.

In Spokane, we met a Christian man who watered the seed that was in my heart. He invited us to an event. As I listened to the speaker, I heard him say things I knew, not anything new. My old misconceptions were right there to negate anything he had to say. But then, he said the one thing I needed to hear. Do you know you can be saved? I had been led to believe that only my compliance with the law would determine my salvation. So, I had concluded that since I could not fully comply with the law, salvation was not possible for me.

Clarity came to my mind as I listened intently to what he said next. He quoted John 3:16. "For God so loved the world that He gave His one and only Son, that whosoever believes in Him shall not perish but have eternal life." He said, "all you have to do is believe in Jesus." With that statement, he told me I did not have to be perfect and I did not have to be in full compliance. I just needed to believe in the Jesus that died for me on the cross. He had set me free from my misconceptions and set me on the path to eternal life with Jesus Christ, my Savior.

More and More of God
By Tabitha Castro

I gave my life to Christ in 2011. I loved God and I honestly wanted to know more about Him every day. About two months into my being saved, I came into a very dark time in my life. I was dealing with depression and anxiety, something I had never dealt with before.

Because I was so new in my salvation and in my relationship with God, I had no idea how to fight in faith. I ended up blaming God for putting me through this and for not listening when I cried out for help. Eventually I stopped praying and reading the Word. I stopped pursuing God completely out of anger and hurt, but I never stopped believing. I was delivered from depression after eight hard and draining months, but by that time I had drifted far from the Lord.

The next four years were the worst of my life. I was living in my own world with my own rules. I had drifted back into my old way of life. And, even though I still believed, I wasn't acting like a believer. I ended up in a relationship with a guy I shouldn't have been with, and because of that, sin had found its way back into my life. I was sleeping with my boyfriend without us being married. I knew we were doing wrong. My conviction brought me to talk to him and we made an effort to stop, only to find ourselves trapped in this cycle. My anxiety and depression returned shortly. I knew it was because of the conflict I was having between what I was doing versus what God wanted me to do. I wanted to stop, but I loved this man so much.

I started going to Faith Assembly around the same time I had been with him. It wasn't often, but every time I went, something in me wanted more and more of God. For years I thought I was okay with my relationship with God; I wasn't reading the Word or praying much, other than to ask for forgiveness every so often. But in my mind, I thought I was doing fine. When I started going to church again, I knew something was off and I wanted to have more of God, but when it came down to God and my boyfriend, I was afraid of letting my boyfriend go.

One night I broke down. I prayed and cried out to God and asked Him what I should do. I called my mom and told her about my relationship with my boyfriend. I was sick of lying to her. Then she told me something that I had never thought about. She said, "God is your husband and He is your matchmaker." I came to the understanding that all this time that I had been asking God what I should do, He had already established it in His Word. That night, I told my boyfriend that either we would get married or we would have to break up. We broke up that night. I had chosen God. Yes, I was heartbroken, but I knew it was for the best.

About a year later, I came to counseling at Faith. Since then, God has truly delivered me from anxiety and depression and I have rededicated my life to God. The road hasn't been easy, but know that I have God by my side...and I can do all things through Christ who strengthens me.

The Pool of Bethesda
By Alberto Davila

In John 5:2-9, we can read about the moment when Jesus healed a man who had been ill for thirty-eight years. I have heard this story before, as you probably have also. For most people, as it was for me, this was just another story about Jesus performing a miracle...until one day; I opened the Bible and began reading the story myself. I read this story and I found myself in it.

In this story, Jesus knew that this man needed healing. God knows everything. So, to me, when Jesus asked him, "Do you want to be healed?", it was a loaded question. I believe what Jesus was actually asking him was, "How bad do you want to be healed? Are you willing to do what it takes to be healed?" The man had been afflicted for years and wanted to be healed. That is why he somehow found his way to the Pool of Bethesda. But, when he answered Jesus, I sensed some hesitation. For some reason, once he found himself so close to the source of healing, he decided to remain there as if he was afraid to commit fully.

As I continued reading this story, I began to weep as I saw myself in it more and more. I was that man. I was spiritually afflicted, so I came to church. I came to Bethesda. I began to participate in the services and would closely listen to the message. I could now see the water so close. I wanted all of God's promises, but I wasn't sure that I was ready to give up other things. For seven years, I continued attending church without being willing to fully commit to giving myself one hundred percent to God.

I used to tell Jesus, "I came this far, now you need to come the rest of the way and meet me here," but then, He opened my heart and showed me that He had already done everything for me when He gave his life on the cross. Just like that man, I knew that I was at the right place. And, I knew what I needed to do. But, something held me back.

After seven years, God put this passage in front of me and opened my eyes. He showed me that for me to be able to claim spiritual healing and all His promises, I would have to commit my life to Him one hundred percent. That day, I got down on my knees and asked God for forgiveness. I thanked him for opening my eyes and for showing me the truth.

One week after that, in March of 2015, I was baptized in water on a Sunday morning. I went into the water, and as I was lifted up…I was finally healed…I was set free.

God is good.

To God Be the Glory
By William Acevedo

By the Grace of God and His mercy, on October 12th, I was able to realize my dream of going on a mission trip. Let me go back in time a bit. In 2005, while trying to complete my physical training to become an Auxiliary Deputy, I was shocked to learn that I had severe rheumatoid arthritis. Shortly after that, I had surgery on both my knees. Unfortunately, I had to discontinue my dream and drop out of the Police Academy. But, the Lord had another purpose for me.

In 2006, I started attending Faith Assembly. And shortly after that, I was born again in Christ. For several years, I had a dream to go on a mission trip abroad. I always had the excuse, I have the time but not the money. Several months before committing to the mission trip, the Lord tugged at my heart and said you are going to the Dominican Republic. I thought, okay, but how? I didn't have the money. Then I said to myself, if the Lord is calling me, I'm going to go. I'm not going to question it. So, I made a commitment to go to the Dominican Republic. Mind you, I was still a little skeptical about my financial situation.

Right after that commitment, the enemy's attacks started. My health began to be an issue. My knees began to hurt and give me a hard time walking. Then, my car was rear-ended. And, six days before leaving for the Dominican Republic, the transmission went out. But I said, "Lord I can't worry about this now. I have to keep my focus on the mission trip."

On October 12th, we left for the Dominican Republic. I started to feel the joy of the Holy Spirit working in us as we boarded the plane. When we reached Cima del Rey, "the mountain of God," we could feel the presence of the Lord and the Holy Spirit. I was told that there was an infamous staircase that leads to the bottom of the mountain, which we had to climb once or twice a day. We got our assignments, praised God, and had supper.

The six days that I was there, I walked up and down that dreaded staircase. It consisted of 107 uneven steps, not to mention the fifty steps to our sleeping quarters, twice a day and sometimes three. But, not once did my knees give me a hard time nor did I feel any pain in all the time I was there.

Our God is awesome. There was joy, love, passion, compassion, unity and anointing. Tears were shed and lives remade. I can't wait to go on my second, and third, and fourth mission trip. I encourage and I challenge you, if you are a Christian, walking the Christ walk. You need to go on a mission's trip. One of my favorite verses is Philippians 4:13, "I can do all things through Christ who strengthens me."

Section III:

*H*EALING

†

"Bless the Lord, O my soul, and forget not all His benefits: who forgiveth all thine iniquities; who healeth all thy diseases."

Psalms 103:2-3 KJV

A Disagreement
By Alex Oliveras

One night when I was 16, I met up with an
acquaintance. We had a disagreement and I went to get my
property out of his vehicle. As I went into the car, he started
to stab me and I began to fight for my life. My hands were
badly cut from defensive wounds and I was stabbed eight
times. I also ended up with a collapsed lung from the
wounds.

I got out of the car and ran to a nearby friend's house
where I sat on his porch bleeding to death. My friend held
my chest because I was losing so much blood. Eventually, I
couldn't see anymore from the blood loss. I felt sleepy, as if I
were going to rest, but I was about to die. As I said my final
goodbyes in my head, and was fading away to die, a jolt of
energy came inside of me and woke me up!

I was taken by ambulance to a helicopter, then to a
hospital that could help. When I arrived at the hospital and
got out of the helicopter, the doctor saw me and said, "He is
not going to make it." I said through the mask, "Don't say
that!" He then looked at me surprised that I spoke!

With God's grace, blood transfusions and surgery, I
made it! People ask how I know it was God? I will explain.
Later, after the whole ordeal, I started serving the Lord. My
church in New Jersey went to a service in New York, and at
the end of the service I went up front for prayer. When the
preacher put his hand on me, a jolt of energy raced through
my body, and I fell. That was confirmation, God telling me
He saved my life. Earlier, I mentioned that when I was about
to die this energy came and woke me up, it was the same
energy I felt when the preacher put his hand on my head. It
was the Holy Spirit of God! Since the ordeal, I faced
depression, PTSD, drug addiction, loneliness, rejection, and
thoughts of suicide. But, nothing is impossible for God! I am
now serving the Lord and happier than I've ever been. He is

the cure to all of our problems if we just give him a chance. Amen!

Daisies
By Pastor Ashley Hawks-VanEst

God's miraculous healing power has manifested in my life many times. One time in particular impacted my faith in God from an early age. I was 5 years old and had just come home from a Daisies class party on a Wednesday night. I was feeling sick to my stomach, which my parents attributed to eating a lot of tasty treats at the party. But, by morning I was running a fever, so my parents took me straight to the doctor who immediately sent me to the ER.

The color had completely drained from my face, and I was terrified! The doctors at the hospital confirmed that I did, in fact, have appendicitis, and they would be doing emergency surgery the next day. My mother started claiming healing over my body, as did my father. Pastor Carl Stephens came to visit me, and he prayed over me as well. By that night, the color had returned to my face, and, for the first time since I had gotten sick, I was hungry and pain-free!

The next day, the nurses did some final pre-surgical tests. The surgeon came to my room dressed in his scrubs and scratching his head. He said he was prepared to do the surgery. They had the OR booked and were ready to go, but my tests from that morning were normal! He could not explain it, but he knew we had a miracle! Since that day, I have never again had a problem with my appendix. I have hung on to this miracle my whole life. It reminds me that whatever I face, our God is the same yesterday, today, and forever. And, He is still doing miracles!

It's Not Over
By Miguel Lopez

On a dark Wednesday night in April 2013, Miguel was in the parking lot of Faith Assembly of God in Orlando, Florida. The Wednesday night service had concluded. Miguel and his brothers, sister in law, family and friends were in earnest prayer for Miguel. Just the Monday before, he had been notified by his doctor that he had three cancerous lumps in his right lung. The doctor felt it was urgent enough to have him scheduled for surgery on Thursday, the next day. As they prayed and asked God to be with Miguel, to give his doctor wisdom and to guide his hands, the lyrics to the song *It's Not Over* came to Miguel's mind:

It's not over! It's not finished!
It's not ending! It's only the beginning.
When God is in it, all things are new.
All things are new!

Miguel's surgeon explained to him that he had three tumors in his lung and they were scattered. The doctor suggested removing his entire infected lung. "You're 59 years old and still young and healthy enough to withstand the surgery. My concern," he told Miguel, "is because of the nature of the surgery and the risk of infection. The best I can offer you is a fifteen to twenty percent survival rate." He was confident Miguel would survive the surgery, but he was worried about the recovery period. "But, that's what I'm saying," said the doctor, "I don't know what the man upstairs has in mind for you." Two days later Miguel found himself being prepared for major surgery.

Miguel's family had been waiting for him in the waiting room. Around 2:00 p.m., the surgeon arrived in the waiting room and said, "Hallelujah, he is cancer free! I have removed his cancer." The surgeon explained that when he operated on Miguel, the three tumors had combined into one. "That is just something that our powerful God does," said the surgeon.

Through this experience, Miguel became convinced of the power of prayer. He tells everyone from all over the country that were praying for him. He is convinced that without the prayers from his friends and family, the outcome would not have been the same. He is confident and steadfast in his belief that prayer has the power to change things.

Miguel has always loved God but now he is attuned to the call of God on his life. He is no longer overly concerned with the cares of this world. He is more concerned with the cares of God. He is aware that the miracle that was performed in his life was not a singular event. He knows God performs miracles every day and the world needs to know that God is alive, working and well. By 2016, Miguel was fully recovered and living a vibrant life for Christ, more in love and excited about Christ than ever before.

It's not over! It's not finished!
It's not ending! It's only the beginning.
When God is in it, all things are new.
All things are new!

Hoops
By Johnnie Wilson

I arrived home after playing some late night basketball on what seemed to be a typical Sunday night back in May of 2005. Following a quick shower, I was sitting on the bed talking with the wife, when numbness started to travel through my whole body. She joked that I was probably having a stroke. I immediately went to the computer to diagnose myself with the help of webMD.com. I couldn't think or see straight as I struggled to type in the words "stroke symptoms." When I finally arrived on the page, most of what I read applied to me. I became less and less coherent. Jamee called some friends to come over and care for our kids, assisted me with what seemed to be the impossible task of putting on a shirt, and then we were off to the hospital.

Most of my experience at the hospital was told to me by others. I was conscious but not able to answer the simplest question. News began to spread quickly through our Faith Assembly of God family and many were already praying for my situation. One of the significant moments I was told about was when one of the doctors spoke up seconds before they administered a blood thinner (a typical treatment for what appeared to be a stroke) because she had "a feeling" that something else was going on. As it turned out, if that blood thinner had been given to me, it would have accelerated and amplified the long-term negative effects of the condition from which I was actually suffering.

I was unconscious for most of the next thirty-six hours. Doctors were trying to run tests and scans while discussing possible theories of what was wrong with me. They were narrowing their diagnosis to things such as viral meningitis, bacterial meningitis, and encephalitis. All of which can carry some serious and lasting complications. At the same time, Christians all over the country were praying for me. The hospital waiting room became a student prayer center as much of the youth group kept streaming through the hospital to pray together. Everything seemed to change dramatically on Tuesday morning. I gained consciousness and felt completely normal! I believe some of my first words were used to request a Coke (a sure sign I was back to my old self again).   They discharged me about twenty-four hours later. I was without symptoms and every test that they had run at that point was normal.

A few weeks later, at a follow up visit with my doctor, he said to me, "we never did figure out what happened to you or how you improved so quickly." He said that he assumed it was encephalitis and or meningitis, but couldn't explain how those things went away on their own. I was able to share my theory as I told him how many people were praying for me to a God who still heals…a God who is present and active in our lives. He had a hard time disagreeing with that!

The Great Healer
By Barbara "Barbie" Burcham

On October 3, 1993, I got a severe headache and was sent to the hospital Intensive Care Unit (ICU). After a brain scan, spinal tap, several Magnetic Resonance Imaging (MRI) scans and an angiogram, I was diagnosed with an aneurysm of the brain on the lower right side of my head. I was scheduled to have surgery on October 7th at 8:00 a.m. Before the surgery, my family and a close friend were called into my room and were informed that I might not make it or that I could become a vegetable for the rest of my life. My doctor, who was also a pastor, began to pray with me by repeating Psalms 23 over and over again.

Around 3:00 a.m., the morning of the surgery, with my head shaved, I woke up with such peace; I could feel warm oil flowing from the top of my head to the bottom of my feet. My head stopped hurting immediately and I felt like I could float. I called the nurse in, and she thought I needed more morphine for the pain, but I told her that I was not going to have surgery because "Jesus had just healed me." She called the doctor in, and I was taken for another MRI, but the blood clot was gone! I went from ICU Critical Care to "discharged to go home" that same day, with the promise that I would return in a week for another MRI. To this day, I have not had a headache, not even a slight one. The Great Healer does the job right the first time. Thank You, Jesus!

Skateboarding
By Gerson Torres

As a visitation pastor, I see a lot of hurting, sorrow and pain. That is the pulpit that I work from weekly. I also get to see God's work in patients in the hospital. One such patient was a young man 18 years of age. This patient was hit while he was on his skate board.

He was crossing the street in Winter Park and a car hit him, he flew 40 feet in the air and landed on his head. He was taken to the hospital with severe head injuries. The doctors performed multiple surgeries, in particular on his brain. His single mom called the hospital asking for prayer for her son.

In this type of accident, the first 72 hours are critical. He was later in ICU for an extended period of time. The doctors had a conference with the mother and informed her that they had done all they could, and concluded her son would not recover. The doctors suggested that he be put in an assisted living facility. The mother refused to accept this suggestion and she asked the doctors to continue looking into other options for her son. She persevered throughout the ordeal and prayed day and night for her son's recovery.

I saw the boy daily during the week and sometimes on weekends. The grace of God slowly began manifesting itself in the life of this patient and he got better and better. Initially his speech was difficult and his gait and walk were challenging. A year later, he was discharged to a rehab center and he improved significantly. The ordeal for this boy was about two years long.

His mom was very grateful for all the prayers offered on his behalf from the people at Faith Assembly. These people didn't know her son. She brought him to Faith Assembly Of God at Goldenrod and he gave his testimony on a Sunday service. Today, he is a vibrant man 24 years of age. God gave me the opportunity to see his mighty works and it brought tears to my eyes. To God be the glory and honor.

BEFORE &

AFTER

✝

"Brethren, I count not myself to have apprehended: but this one thing I do, forgetting those things which are behind, and reaching forth unto those things which are before. I press toward the mark for the prize of the high calling of God in Christ Jesus."

Philippians 3:13-14 KJV

God Comforts the Depressed
By Brandi Gladney

In just ten years, 23 times I received news that a loved one had died. Five times cancer struck our family, three times cardiovascular disease, multiple sclerosis, thyroid disease, stillborn babies, diabetes, tragic accidents, substance abuse, even murder. As life moves us further apart, supporting one another has proven to be extremely difficult. Sadly, many of the remaining relationships have been tainted by the coldness of apathy and fed by the misery of unmet needs from our youth to this day.

These last ten years have been both lonely and full of grief. My heart has ached so deeply that it hurt to breathe. I have been weary, sick and heartbroken. I was afflicted on every side: conflicts on the outside, fears within. Anger started to rise up and I began to question the God I thought I knew. How could a loving God allow this? Consumed with loss, death and grief, anger began chipping away at my faith.

Much of my anger was wrongfully directed at God for allowing so much loss and pain. I looked for relief in my family, my friends, my work, shopping and traveling. But, I found no rest. One by one, each of these things let me down. Conflict seemed to follow me wherever I went, although I desperately wanted peace. My relationships were more strained and distant. Tempers seemed to flare up over just about anything. I was deeply bruised and my heart ached even more. So, I turned back to the throne of grace, still angry, but needing God's rest.

I was always honest with God, often apologizing for being so irrationally angry with Him. When I couldn't pray, I would ask Jesus and the Holy Spirit to pray for me. And slowly but surely, with time, I began to speak the Word of God, which will never come back void. "Peace I leave with you, my peace I give unto you: not as the world giveth, give I unto you. Let not your heart be troubled, neither let it be afraid (John 14:27)." The Holy Spirit was softening my heart and ministering to me.

Rarely has a night gone by that I haven't prayed for each and every one of us that is grieving the loss of a loved one. But God, who comforts the depressed, comforted me (2 Corinthians 7:5-6). And, through my prayers and His Word, I trust He has comforted you too. I have learned that there are clear and present dangers among our loved ones, and certainly, dangers in this fallen world. And, believe me, I have searched far and wide. There is no rest in mankind.

"My soul finds rest in God alone; my salvation comes from Him. He alone is my rock and my salvation; He is my fortress, I will never be shaken (Psalm 62:1-2)."

God Wants to Give Us the Desires of Our Hearts
By Cary Petiot

When my daughter was around 13 or 14, she and I participated in a home Bible study. It was just what we needed because my husband, her father, had recently left and we were going through some rough times. Christmas was quickly coming, and my finances were almost nonexistent. My dear daughter was trying to make life easier for me, so she came to me and shared that she just wanted one gift for Christmas. She was used to multiple gifts and felt that by only requesting one, she was taking the stress off me. I asked and she shared that she was teaching herself to play the keyboard by ear, but her keyboard was too small. She wanted a large professional type. My heart broke as I knew that there was no way I could afford that. She understood and said she was sorry for asking. I cried and I prayed, and told her how sorry I was, and how I wished I could get it for her.

Fast forward to the Bible study. The couple that led the group had just lost their jobs and were also struggling. Their church blessed them with their next month's rent and a food basket. They were so overwhelmed that they wanted to bless someone else but could not figure out what they could do. The wife remembered something that her mother had given her a couple of years before that was still in its original box in their closet. They knew that this is what they had to gift someone. They prayed that the Lord would show them who He wanted them to bless. My name kept coming up, but this baffled them, as they really did not know a lot about me. They called me, however, to see if something would be revealed to them. As soon as they started speaking to me, they realized that it was not for me but for my daughter Nicole. They questioned me to see if Nicole had asked for anything in particular for Christmas. I said yes but I could not afford it, and I was not about to tell them about my need as they had just lost their job. I was still in the dark about what was happening. I did not want to share, but they were very insistent, so I told them about the keyboard. Now they knew for sure.

Christmas Eve arrived and so did this couple. As they stood at the door, I called Nicole and told her someone was there to see her. There stood David and Dinah holding a box with a professional, full-size keyboard. Along with the keyboard was a set of beginner instruction books. The Lord does not do things halfway. He had something for me as well. Included was a headset that Nicole could wear while playing so no one else would hear the music. Praise God! He is so good! The keyboard had been in her closet for two years and had never been touched.

Nicole was amazed and had a smile from ear to ear. We both realized just how much the Father loves us and wants to give us the desires of our hearts. This moment had been orchestrated by God years before Nicole even requested it. Amazing! Let us never underestimate our Father's love.

100%
By Dondi Sanchez

When I got saved in 1994, my family and I quickly became members of Faith Assembly of God. We were required to sign some paperwork stating we understood and agreed with Faith Assembly of God's beliefs. There was one particular section about paying tithes. We had to sign this page agreeing to pay our tithe weekly. I could not agree, because I was self-employed and had only been working in my field for a few years. We had just bought a house and we had a child. I just couldn't agree to pay my tithe every week especially since we only got paid every 30 days. So, I just skipped that part and handed it in.

A couple of days later, I received a call from the pastor who taught the membership class. I explained my personal situation and told him that I didn't believe that God would keep me from heaven just because I didn't pay my tithe faithfully. The pastor agreed, but he told me that God wants to know that we will give him full authority over every aspect of our lives. I told him I understood what he was saying, but I still couldn't accept it. I just kept doing what I was doing in our lives and finances, paying our tithe whenever we could.

No matter how hard I tried to make things work on my own, thinking I didn't need God to be part of my finances, it didn't work. The day it all changed for me, Pastor Carl was teaching on tithing. He said, "if you want the full blessing of God, if you want to receive everything He desires to give you, you have to give Him complete control over every area of your life" and yes, that included my finances. He explained that God would be faithful to me if I were faithful to Him in every area of my life. He would provide for our every need, but He would provide in a measure unequal to our commitment. He would out give us in every aspect of our lives.

I remember feeling inadequate because no matter what I did, I couldn't do it on my own. I made a choice to give my finances over to God. I remember telling God right then and there that I gave him full control over my finances and I would tithe no matter what. I immediately started paying my tithes. Things started getting easier. We started having money in the bank. We started having money for other things. Don't get me wrong; it was still hard at times. But, I didn't have that fear of what we were going to do or what was going to happen. Instead, I just kept trusting God.

There have been times when I was sitting paying bills, writing our tithe check, and I would look at the amount and I'd be like, wow! If this is something you are struggling with, just give it over to God. Trust Him. Have faith in Him. Trust God in every aspect of your life and see all the blessings that He has in store for you.

Less and More
By Israel Pagan

While watching a TV show one morning, I saw a woman selected from the crowd. She was in her sixties and poorly dressed. In a few hours, her hair was dyed and styled, her face etched with makeup and she was dressed in nice clothing. She looked totally different, at least ten years younger, and said she felt better than ever before. It's easy to have a makeover, a before and after, but if you don't maintain it, chances are, your old appearance will resurface.

I've had a few makeovers in my life. As a young teenager, I was addicted to drugs and as an adult I succumbed to alcohol. My physical appearance and lifestyle were deplorable. I detoxed in hospitals, rehab centers and correctional facilities. And, I looked and felt better. But in a few weeks, I was back to my old self. Just like the woman's makeover, I could have stayed clean and sober, but it required time and effort in order to achieve permanent results. I somehow managed to survive and after living clean and sober for many years, I've often asked myself the question: Have I really experienced a true "before and after"?

During a sermon one Sunday morning in church, I heard the pastor say, "God's blessings are constant, but for some reason, we just fail to see them." Although I'd heard this before, this time it was an awakening and the concept of before and after Christ took on a new meaning. I thought before Christ meant He wasn't present in my life when I needed Him the most, and that I had conquered my demons on my own. I now realize He was always with me, which explains why I didn't die of an overdose or in a car accident while driving intoxicated. It's a humbling experience to truly understand and believe it was all Jesus, and that I had very little, if anything, to do with my recovery. But what about my life after Christ? I thought this meant that my life would be on some kind of spiritual cruise control. I now realize that although I'm doing much better, I must continue to do my share if I'm to understand His will and purpose for my life.

Understanding my life before and after Christ is a true blessing. It reconciles my past, helps me better understand the present and provides perspective for the future. More importantly, it clarifies the misconception that I was loved less before Christ and more after Christ. This can't be further from the truth. "But God demonstrates his own love for us in this: while we were still sinners, Christ died for us" (Romans 5:8). That's why I must continue to believe in His Word and seek His will as I strive for a life of meaning and purpose. Because if I don't, it will be just like the woman's makeover—I will look and feel better for a while, only to return to a life of despair.

"PAPI, Where Are You?"
By Odette Del Río

It may not mean much to those whose daddy has always been there for them, but I had been praying for years in my search for *Papi* from the age of four. The Yellow Cab pulled away on Taylor Street and my hand reached out for my *Papi,* looking out the back window, as he got smaller and smaller until he was no more. From then on, my little heart grieved for him.

The years went by as I was tossed about many different households. I attended 23 different schools and lived in Illinois, New York City, St. Croix, Puerto Rico, back to New York City, and under miraculous circumstances, returned to Puerto Rico. All the while, I needed my dad to be a part of my life, especially at key moments. On February 18, 1973, in Puerto Rico, I had a life changing experience after pouring my entire being into my Lord Jesus Christ at a youth evangelistic service one Sunday afternoon at a United Methodist Church.

Upon moving to Orlando, Florida, things were not turning out as I believed they would. My biological father was not on my mind because of impending, critical situations. Prayer led me to my Heavenly Father who had never forsaken me no matter how my circumstances looked. Relying on Him was best, for I had no one else. I can look back and clearly know I indeed had it all because He was always with me. I could not do anything but trust Him completely, and I rested on Him.

Within a week of arriving in Florida, I was in possession of a driver's license, a good car, proper auto insurance, plus a job I held for the following 20 years. Looking back again, the Lord worked all things out perfectly for me.

My father was on my mind again, and I diligently searched for him every possible way I could. Later, a coworker's daughter, who lived in Chicago, located his address and shared it with me. I wrote to him and included my contact information. He called me, and we spoke for almost 2 hours. It was Father's Day! Delightfully, we spoke again on Monday about life events. I called him back on Tuesday, but his telephone number was disconnected. I wrote, but the letters were returned to me. Once again, the door had been closed.

Recently my husband was channel flipping, and we were drawn to the TV program: "Long Lost Family." I knew of a similar program called "The Locator", but this one prompted my husband to Google my maiden name. He found someone with that name and asked me if I knew her. I said, "Yes! That's my dad's wife." He informed me that it was an obituary and she had died less than two months prior.

This is the beginning of my next *Papi* chapter. We are now in communication and soon to meet. For my Living God has responded to my prayers. "When my father and my mother forsake me, then the LORD will take care of me." (Psalm 27:10)

Anger

By Raymond Peoples

Before Christ, I was a two-headed coin. On one side of the coin: a pleasant, humble, gentle and kind man. On the other: I was easily angered and filled with uncontrollable meanness. So uncontrolled, that there was no regret, no conviction, and no remorse.

God needed to get my attention, but having a mind full of turmoil made hearing his voice impossible. An intervention was needed and through two heartbreaks, things began to change. The first resulted in days of indescribable thoughts and confusion; I was a wanderer searching for answers. Then, on Good Friday many years ago, I ended up in the parking lot of an Episcopal church. That was the day my heart began to change, and the Word of God became alive in me.

Years later, emotional turmoil still existed and was wreaking havoc on my family, and once again, God needed to intervene directly. As I watched my family walk out the door and the tears flowed, I knew I needed help. God's grace and mercy guided me to an amazing counselor and a men's church group. Through counseling, I could fully understand where all my anger originated and how it hindered my personal life.

I knew what made a man in my mind and though I had it all, I never felt like one. I would hear, "this is what men do" from my wife constantly and would burst out in anger. She didn't know the pain it caused me; no man would ever tell a woman that he doesn't feel like a man.

Through the men's group, I learned that many in the group faced the same challenges. They shared their stories, and I shared mine; glory to God that I wasn't alone in what I was feeling and the man within me finally arose.

Today God's mighty hand and strength governs my behavior and thoughts. Do I still fail today with my anger and emotions? Absolutely, I'm still human with some immature emotions, but now, I get deeply saddened for any pain I cause, and I'm aware of when I need to step back and settle my mind. I thank God that I'm not the person I used to be. When I see myself in the mirror and ask, "Who are you?" My answer is always, "a child of the Most High God." I thank God for never abandoning me and for His continued blessings.

Big and Small
By Gerald Presley

My wife lost her wedding band and was very upset, we looked everywhere but could not find it, after dinner, we looked some more but still couldn't find it. Then it came to me why didn't we pray, so we said a prayer "God, please help us find the ring it means so much to her, please help us, and we give you all the glory."

I went to pick up my meds and by the time I got back she had the ring on her finger. I ask where was it and she said "don't ask," well all that matters is that God answers prayer. She told me later she found it in her bra how it got there we are not sure. All I know is God wants to be in our life for the big things and the small. He Loves us and is always looking for ways to bless us. All we have to do is ask, don't be upset if the answer is no; because He sees the big picture and knows what is best for us all. TO GOD BE THE GLORY FOREVER AND EVER...

Section V:

CONCLUSION

✝

"And they overcame him by the blood of the Lamb, and by the word of their testimony; and they loved not their lives unto the death."

Revelation 12:11 KJV

Prayer of Salvation

If after reading these testimonies, you find yourself in a place in your life where you are not sure if you have a relationship with our Lord Jesus or that you are saved, this is an excellent opportunity to give your life to God. Ask God to come into your heart, and to forgive and cleanse you from all of your sins.

Please write your prayer of repentance below or just say the following:

Dear Lord Jesus,

I know that I am a sinner and I ask for Your forgiveness. I believe You died for my sins and rose from the dead. I turn from my sins and invite You to come into my heart and life. I want to trust and follow You as my Lord and Savior. In Jesus' Name.

Amen.

If you choose to use your own words, please follow the basic principles of the prayer above.

If you prayed to receive salvation, please let us know by emailing or calling us at:

Faith Assembly of God (407) 275-8790

Acknowledgement

I would like to thank all of the people that submitted their testimonies. Please know that your testimonies have made an impact on my life and in the lives of the other writers involved in this project. Thank you Pastor Carl Stephens and Pastor Lester Rector for your leadership and commitment to this effort. And, a special thank you to all of the Faith Assembly of God staff members for your support and contributions.

I would like to thank Mrs. Brandi Gladney and Mrs. Maria Bozcar, our Editors, for their valuable wisdom and input. Without their attention to detail and their knowledge of the English language, this book would not have been possible.

Finally, I would like to thank and acknowledge the Writers of Faith. These individuals have been instrumental in the concept, design and collection of all the necessary information in the production of this book. They all invested many hours into the writing process. Thank you, Mr. Alberto Davila, Mrs. Migdalia Maldonado, Miss Jaquatta Simmons, Miss Gabriela Triyono and Mrs. Brandi Gladney. We sincerely thank the spouses of everyone involved for understanding our passion to write this book.

I sincerely thank you all.

Ruben Figueroa

ABOUT THE AUTHORS
Writers of Faith

We are a team of individuals who have the passion to share the gospel through our gifts of writing. We come together to share our talents and to help one another grow in the purpose God has given us. Although we all have the gift of writing, God has given us unique voices in our writing to touch lives. Our mission is to help and encourage writers to develop their gift of writing for the glory of God.

If after reading these testimonies, you would like to share yours, we encourage you to. Please write your testimony and send it to https://writersoffaithof.wordpress.com/testimonies-of-faith/ or scan this barcode. You can also email your testimony to lbfaithrf@gmail.com.

If you would like to leave a review or a comment, please send it to lbfaithrf@gmail.com.

On behalf of all who participated in this project, we would like to thank you for reading it.

Faith Groups

By Ruben Figueroa

Some of you may have heard of small groups, but are not quite sure what they are. The best way to describe them is to share my experience. We, my wife and I, have attended Faith Assembly of God for a long time. As a matter of fact, both of our daughters graduated from Faith Christian Academy. That, in short, is how we ended up at Faith. I would say we attended for more than ten years before we became involved in small groups.

It was Migdalia Maldonado who persistently invited us to check out the bowling team that exposed us to small groups. We finally went, and we have enjoyed bowling for the past two years. We enjoy the competition and the games. But, it really isn't the bowling that keeps us coming back. It's the people we have met and made close connections with. We look forward to going out together for a few hours every week to have some fun.

Shortly after we joined the bowling league, I decided to start my own small group, the Writers of Faith. This book is a result of our collaboration. Later on, I joined the Faith Business Group; I am a business owner, and I was hoping I could get help, while being helpful to other Christian business owners.

Recently, another member, David, started a small group called "Dominoes for Jesus." We play dominoes and share the Word of God twice a month. My wife and I have volunteered in the Fall Festival. And most recently, I helped with the Thanksgiving outreach. We have attended the God Encounters. And, I have returned to be a group leader for the Men's God Encounter. No one has twisted my arm or tried to manipulate me into investing my time. I have found it to be a blessing to me to be involved in these groups at Faith.

By participating in the small groups at Faith Assembly of God, you will be doing as Pastor Lester Rector always says, "doing life together." You can find a group at Faith for just about any interest. And if you can't, you may be able to start one. God never intended for you to be an island. Whether in business or life, you are part of the body, and you need to connect. We can accomplish great things faster and better when we share the gifts God has given us one with another. I encourage you to check out a small group. You will find it to be more of a blessing than you expected. If you wish to check out a small group at Faith Assembly, please call or visit the website.

Faith Assembly of God (407) 275-8790

http://faithassembly.org/faithgroups/

Faith Groups

Testimony Pages

Please use these pages to write your testimony even if you don't share it with us, please share it with someone.

*The chemistry between us
was undeniable...*

To the readers who fell in love with Jax
and wanted to see him get his HEA.